THE MANY FACES OF COURAGE

Sometimes you will fight your way through
Battle after battle and show your strength and
Courage by being a *warrior*.

Sometimes you will wait, listen to your heart,
Find wisdom to take the right path, and show your strength and
Courage by being *patient*.

Sometimes you will stand up for what you believe in,
Say "no" to that which is not compatible with
Your values, and show your strength and
Courage by being *true to yourself*.

Sometimes you will open new doors for yourself
Even when you seem too tired to go on.

You will find the energy to see a new dawn,
A new point of view, and create a new direction
Where none seems possible.
You will show your strength and courage by being *optimistic*...

But no matter how many times you are knocked down,
With strength and courage *you will always rise again*.

--Bonnie St. John

FOREWORD

You can't know what you don't know, but what you don't know can cost you and your family enormously... emotionally and financially.

Kim Scouller, an attorney with Jade Law Offices of Atlanta, puts it this way: "What people need to know is there are basically two types of lawyers: 'litigators' and 'negotiators.' With litigators, the outcome is a winner and a loser, and the focus is on winning at the cost of the other side. With negotiators, the outcome is a winner and a winner, and their focus is on finding a solution that meets the needs of all sides."

Bottom line, the litigation-focused divorce attorneys will cost a family $30,000 to $100,000 (often more), while the negotiation-oriented attorneys will cost a family $3,000-$15,000 for an average divorce case.

The Transitions Resource workbook provides a step-by-step process of gathering together, in one place, everything you need to know and do to prepare relevant, essential evidence for settlement negotiations and make an outline for financial freedom once your divorce is finalized. This same evidence is also critical in minimizing the length of a litigated case and the likelihood of a very costly—and often fruitless—court trial.

"Very few people are happy they went to court," says divorce attorney Randall M. Kessler, 2011-2012 Chair of the Family Law Section of the American Bar Association, founder of Kessler & Solomiany of Atlanta, and author of Divorce: Protect Yourself, Your Kids, and Your Future (due out March 2013). "They're out all that money. The judge never understands the whole situation and they never get it exactly right."

Kessler agrees the more you know, both about the facts about your household and how the divorce system works, the more successful your mediation will be. In any divorce, "There's a risk you'll be taken advantage of, and the main thing is to make sure you have all the information," he says. "Get the facts. How much money is there? Where is it? What is there to divide?"

"You must have some idea of the laws in your state," he goes on. "Educate yourself about what the divorce legal system looks like from the inside. Find the child support guidelines online. Find out how property is divided in your state."

Putting emotions aside is a tough proposition in the throes of any divorce, but getting the specifics down is the key. This workbook makes this daunting process simple, breaking it into manageable small steps so your true financial and living situation, and your goals, will emerge.

A parallel exercise Kessler recommends is to "step outside of your shoes and pretend it's a friend's divorce. What do you think is fair? Nine times out of 10, it's going to be a close approximation," he says. "Generally, this is common-sense. When you're being objective, you can see all the reasonable possibilities."

A huge mistake many divorcing spouses make, and which some attorneys exploit by not setting them straight, is they think the judge needs to hear all the evidence they've gathered against the spouse, and the minute details of the personal situation, how the spouse has been wronged, et cetera. "The judge will not care about all the inside information you're harboring," Kessler says. "This is not about that. It's about solving a problem. How do two households live on the same funds as the original one?" For instance, a central problem in most divorces is to figure out how children will spend quality time with both parents. "Solve that problem, solve the financial situation. It doesn't help to draw it out."

Lastly, and perhaps most importantly, aside from getting all the facts down, is realize people are people, and appeal to their human nature. "One thing that I always try to convey to my clients is that people are less likely to do things because they have to, and more likely to do things because they want to," Kessler says. "You have to ask them, not force them. Make people *want* to do things. Litigation makes them *have* to do it. Mediation makes them *want* to do it. Wouldn't you rather face something that you want to do, rather than something you have to do?"

Mediation-focused attorneys regard court as a last resort, only warranted when absolutely necessary. Gathering emotionally-fueled facts beyond the basic, problem-solving data, the latter of which this workbook lays down, is a waste of time and money. Divorce insiders know this. Feelings and emotional pain simply do not count in the courtroom.

By adhering closely to this workbook, which will help you get down the facts, analyze them, and strive for the win-win, you will be able to preserve resources that would be wasted in a court of law, and instead use them to go on with your life and provide for your family's future. Moreover, this specific information creates a segueway into a less tangible yet critical aspect of divorce, which is this: the less conflict a divorce sustains, the easier it is to move on in your co-parenting and your broader life. High-conflict divorces inflict deep wounds that particularly cripple parenting attempts, and constantly get in the way of efforts to foster the well-being of the children.

Perhaps the greatest advantage a mediation-focused divorce can offer extends beyond the financial. Mediation, as opposed to a bloody courtroom battle that leaves one winner and often both sides destitute, greatly increases the chances that the former spouses can settle into a civil, productive co-parenting relationship post-divorce, which naturally extends to family, friends, even co-workers.

Like it or not, your actions--and reactions—in perhaps the most tumultuous time in your life will set your family's course for the future. Let this workbook be your roadmap.

Janie McQueen
Author

Janie McQueen is a longtime journalist for major metro newspapers including The Atlanta Journal-Constitution, and the author of four books, including a widely praised self help guide on divorce gamesmanship and its impact on women *Hanging On By My Fingernails, Surviving The New Divorce Gamesmanship And How A Scratch Can Land You In Jail*. Having experienced a contentious divorce herself in the past six years, she is well aware of the landmines that lie along the modern divorce landscape, and is devoted to educating others so they can avoid being victimized by ever-vicious legal traps and ploys. The mother of four, she is happily remarried and lives in metro Atlanta. www.JanieMcQueen.com

TABLE OF CONTENTS

Average Time Line of Divorce Process	7
Gathering Financial Information for Settlement Negotiations	8
Preparing for Financial Independence	11
Consideration of Family Home	12
Establish Custodial Logs for Minor Children	13
When Domestic Violence is an Element in Your Case	14
Securing A Negotiation Style Attorney	16
Consideration of Mediation versus Litigation/Trial	18
How to Tell The Children	19
List of Documents to Gather– Exhibit A	23
Family Monthly Budget Worksheet	25
Family Asset/Net Worth Worksheet	27
Financial Considerations Regarding Divorce Settlements	28
Sample Parenting Plan – Exhibit B	32
Resources	39

AVERAGE TIMELINE OF DIVORCE PROCESS

Prep for Case	Securing Counsel	Negotiation	Mediation	Hearing
Establish records, logs and evidence (Transitions Workbook)	Interview candidates Select Counsel	Negotiate btwn Opposing Counsel 1-4 weeks	1, 2, 3 sessions 4-8 weeks	Hearing Date Established Evidence Prepared Depositions Taken Hearing conducted
		Prep of Settlement Documents/filing 2-5 weeks	Prep of Settlement Documents/filing 2-5 weeks	
		If no resolution reached then Mediations req'd	If no resolution reached then Hearing req'd	
6-24 months	2-3 weeks	3-9 weeks	6-13 weeks	2-6 months **
Average fees	($2500-$5000) retainer due for initial negotiations		($2500-$8000)	($5000-$50,000)

** Final Judgment and Divorce Decree Issued

3 weeks-10 months depending on jurisdiction (county case is filed in) and caseload of Judge

TO-DO ACTION ITEMS

30-60 Days Prior To Securing Attorney

- ❏ Immediately stop talking about separation or divorce
- ❏ Store these materials in a safe keeping place outside of the home. Establish a Safety Deposit Box at a new Bank or store them at a friend or family members' home that is not a friend of your spouse

Gathering Financial Information for Settlement Negotiations:

- ❏ Be aware that any assets you inherit should always be kept separate and in your name only, if you co-mingle them with any assets you acquired during the marriage they will not be exempt from equal distribution. Make sure your Will addresses where these assets should go due to an untimely death. Update your Will immediately if you expect to receive any inheritance prior to the process.

- ❏ Start a monthly log of all household expenditures, a sample log is included

- ❏ Copy all important documents (see list Exhibit A) and create a notebook organizing them. Store the originals and the notebook of copies in a safe keeping place outside of the home.

- ❏ Run an Equifax Credit Report on your family to determine all outstanding accounts and status (seek advice from Counsel before confronting spouse on any new information)

- ❏ Obtain a professional background check on yourself, spouse and children. One can be purchased on-line (see resources). If a general check notes anything suspicious, seek a thorough in-depth background check from a private detective agency if your Attorney advises it at your initial consultation. Do not incur this expense unless advised to as some information is not relevant for the financial or custodial settlement process. Post office boxes or unfamiliar addresses that appear on the background check are an indication that mail relating to hidden assets such as investments and/or banking accounts may be delivered to the address. Sometimes adults place hidden assets under a minor child's name. *Do not confront spouse upon discovery-wait, be patient and allow Counsel to address the appropriate time/method to handle. Keep multiple copies of all evidence documentation in a safe place outside the home.

©2010 Transitions Resource | All rights reserved

If there are suspicious behaviors that your Attorney advises be documented, hire a Private Detective to investigate and document behaviors (DO NOT INVESTIGATE YOURSELF).* If you investigate yourself, this evidence will likely not be substantial to hold up in a court case and it could be defined as stalking and used against you. A professional third party, non-related to the spouse should document the behavior and can testify on your behalf if necessary. This evidence needs to be recent (within 6-9 months) in order to likely hold up in a court case. Do not incur this expense unless your Attorney advises it is necessary. *Do not confront spouse upon discovery-wait, be patient and allow Counsel to address the appropriate time/method to handle. Keep multiple copies of all evidence documentation in a safe place outside the home.

- ❏ If your Attorney advises it, have family computer professionally analyzed (only if necessary). Unusual and/or addictive behaviors can all be documented by a Forensic Computer Analyst who can testify in court on your behalf. *Do not confront spouse upon discovery-wait, be patient and allow Counsel to address the appropriate time/method to handle. Keep multiple copies of all evidence documentation in a safe place outside the home.

- ❏ Make sure your name is on all deeds and titles of any assets that were acquired during the marriage, and that you are listed as beneficiary on any Life Insurance Spouse holds.

- ❏ If family financials are complicated, or you suspect there are hidden or moved family assets, hire a Forensic Accountant to find your hidden assets. If your spouse has placed security passwords on financial, utility and cell phone accounts that you do not know, it is likely there are hidden assets you are unaware of.

Seek financial advice from a Professional Accountant regarding recommended financial settlement. There may be tax implications regarding dividing certain assets. When negotiating a financial settlement take into consideration the value of pre-tax assets versus after-tax assets, retirement accounts are worth less money dollar-for-dollar than cash or liquid accounts because they will be taxed later.

Some individuals do not realize that alimony is taxable, so it is important to understand what your ultimate tax liability would be as a divorced status when you are negotiating the financial settlement.

❑ Get Insurance Coverage Quotes:

Medical Insurance

Contact your current Medical Insurance provider and Prescription Medication provider and have them mail you a detailed itemization of your past usage and claims for the last 12-18 months. Take this information to an independent Medical Benefits broker and get 2 separate quotes (1) coverage for yourself alone; (2) coverage for you and including any minor children you have. This information will be needed for your financial settlement negotiation. If you suspect that when you are divorced you will need an insurance plan with a $5000 deductible or more, and your adjusted gross income is taxable, see your local Banker to establish a "Health Savings Account" (HSA) that allows you to claim your out-of-pocket medical expenses to be tax free. Once your HSA is established, you may want to negotiate with your spouse which of you will continue to fund this account to get the tax-free write off on taxes each year

Consider COBRA coverage, if available through your soon to be ex-spouse's employer group. A Qualified Beneficiary who loses group medical and/or dental coverage due to a qualifying event, such as a divorce, may elect to continue the group medical and/or dental coverage for 36 months on a self-pay basis. Contact the HR Department at the company and request that the COBRA packet be forwarded to you at your current address. You have 60 days from the date of the qualifying event to elect COBRA.

A single parent should consider supplemental medical insurance such as AFLAC. A medical emergency or an unexpected medical expense could financially devastate your ability to provide for yourself or minors. Obtain a quote for these expenses and consider this expense when negotiating your final financial settlement.

Auto Insurance

Get a quote for yourself as a single driver policy and a quote for yourself and any minor children in your household who are driving or may be driving within the upcoming years. This information should be taken into consideration regarding expenses for child support and alimony settlement negotiations.

Home Owners Insurance or Renters Insurance

Get a quote for a policy based on the home situation you intend to pursue once your case is settled. This information should be taken into consideration regarding expenses for child support and alimony settlement negotiations.

See Attachments in back of workbook titled "Financial Considerations for Divorce Settlements" for a more in depth discussion on items to consider with a Professional Financial Advisor before entering financial negotiations.

Preparing For Financial Independence:

- ❏ After your filing, during a temporary settlement phase and prior to reaching settlement, have your Spouse be required to add your name to all utility bills (phone, T.V. cable, Internet, gas, electric, water); this is essential in order to avoid large deposits required when opening new accounts when you separate. Have your name added to all investment accounts (stocks, bonds). If your name is not on the investment accounts when separating the marital assets through your settlement, you could incur substantial tax liability (28-35% short term capital gains) should you need to sell them within 12 months of the funds being separated. Always seek advice from a CPA who is IRS certified before moving any of these assets.

- ❏ Try to resolve all debt on joint account credit cards:
  - ○ Remove spouse from any credit cards that you are Primary holder/Spouse is authorized user (if possible without suspicion)
  - ○ Remove yourself from any joint credit cards where Spouse is Primary holder/you are authorized user (if possible without suspicion)

- ❏ Seek employment, full or part-time if not employed, as soon as possible. Judges likely will not rule favorably toward an individual who initiates the divorce process without a clear plan in terms of providing for themselves independently (should your case require a hearing).

- ❏ Establish your own banking savings/checking accounts at a different bank (without Spouse's name on them). DO NOT HAVE THE STATEMENTS MAILED TO YOUR HOME, you can rent a mail box at local UPS Stores or the Post Office where these can be mailed.

- ❏ Start to establish independent credit history, apply for at least 2 credit cards alone based on your current family income and credit history (it will be very important for your financial survival later to have this established credit in your name only, you may need to put legal fees on them or use them initially for monthly expenses). DO NOT HAVE THESE STATEMENTS MAILED TO YOUR HOME. Make a few charges each month on these cards and pay them off 100% on time by the required due date every month.

Consideration of the Family Home:

Your family home may be the most valuable family asset you have to address in your financial settlement. Many divorcing individuals want to stay in the family home after the divorce is final. Some consideration should be given to what other possibilities you may have. Agreeing to sell the family home, split the proceeds and downsizing to a smaller/less expensive living arrangement can be a freeing experience, both financially and emotionally. If you decide to keep and stay in the home as your part of the financial settlement, you may find yourself under enormous financial pressure. Consider all of the expenses of taking on the home ownership versus renting a house or townhome:

Ownership
Mortgage payment (can your income qualify for a loan as a borrower with your lender?)
Home Owner Insurance
Utilities of a large dwelling (may be more room than you actually need)
Home Owner Association dues
Taxes
Upkeep, maintenance and expenses related to appliances, HVAC, Hot Water Heater, roof, etc.

Renting
Rent
Rental Insurance
Utilities of a smaller dwelling

Many individuals have been happy to liquidate this valuable asset, pad their bank account and reduce their financial obligations as they seek financial independence.

Brad Burns, Certified Divorce Financial Analyst , Certified Distressed Property Expert offers the following options:

When a property has equity and payments are current:
A. List for Sale and divide net proceeds after tax and other costs
B. Refinance the Mortgage and seek additional funds for one party to reimburse other for their share of equitable interest
C. One party retains and chooses to occupy if they can afford the home expenses once divorce is final
D. Agree to sell at a future date while one party or a Qualified Lessee occupies the house
E. One party retains ownership while the other party rents from the retaining party, this option can have tax advantages for one party which should be considered in overall settlement

When a property has negative equity and is possibly in distress:
A. Enter into a Short Sales agreement with the lender. In this case it is possible to avoid foreclosure, consult a CDPE for advice
B. Modif the loan through the lender and utilize government programs if qualified to make payments to avoid foreclosure
C. List for Lease to help maintain the mortgage if neither party can afford to remain in the home

Brad P. Burns, CDFA, CFA, CDPE   (770) 380-2406

Establish Custodial Logs if you have minor children still living with you:

This step is very important as this documentation can be used as supporting evidence to eliminate a custody battle, do not overlook the value of establishing these records.

- ❏ Start a daily log/journal of all activities you do with children, separate log of spouse's activities with children and keep in a safe place (make sure this includes school visits, medical visits, sports, extracurricular activities). If your spouse travels often for employment, it is important to document details of the frequency of travel and time-away from the children with travel itineraries, flight and hotel receipts, credit card charges out-of-town. This will establish a history of primary care-taking on your part.

- ❏ Eliminate personal vulnerabilities that would make you appear as an unfit parent in the eyes of a Judge, seek counseling or support groups. This includes eliminating daily or regular use of alcohol and/or narcotic prescription medications as discussed with your prescribing Physician. Make sure that friends and family members are aware of these changes in your habits in case you need to secure affidavits from them in the future.

Start to document Spouse's vulnerabilities for custody if there are minor children involved. Collect receipts of expenditures (or credit card bills) to document frequent purchases of alcohol or medications. Medical Prescription/ Insurance Claims history are also adequate documentation as evidence. Your local Pharmacy can run accumulative reports of medical prescriptions filled by your family. This evidence needs to be recent to actual filing (6-9 months within filing) in order to likely hold up in a court case. If you suspect there will be a potential custody battle, it is well-worth the investment for a professional investigator to document the vulnerabilities of your spouse, otherwise it is likely to be perceived as a "He-said/She said" scenario which is difficult to prove to a Judge. Hard documented evidence by an outside party will likely encourage opposing counsel to settle custody issues out of court. State Codes in Domestic Law usually address the following regarding Custodial Responsibility:

Parents' Obligation to Child

It is the joint and several duty of each parent to provide for the maintenance, protection, and education of his or her child until the child reaches the age of majority, dies, marries or becomes emancipated, whichever first occurs, except as otherwise authorized and ordered as further defined by court order.

Criteria for Loss of Parental Custody

If a child is found under circumstances of destitution and suffering, abandonment, or exposure or if the child has been begging or if it is found that the child is being reared under immoral, obscene, or indecent influences which are likely to degrade his moral character and devote him to a vicious life and it appears to the appropriate court by competent evidence including such examination of the child as may be practicable, that by reason of the neglect, habitual drunkenness, lewd or other vicious habits, or other behavior of the parents or guardians of the child, it is necessary for the welfare of the child to protect the child from such conditions, the court may order that the parents or guardians be deprived of custody of the child and that appropriate measures as provided by law be taken for the welfare of the child.

When domestic violence is an element in your case:

What is domestic violence? If your spouse, partner, family member or caretaker:

hits, slaps, punches, chokes, kicks, pushes, shoves or spits on you; threatens or scares you with a weapon; forces or coerces you to have sex when you don't want to; threatens to take away your children; blames you for his/her violent behavior; withholds affection as punishment; takes away your money, house keys or car keys; keeps you from seeking medical attention; says that you deserve to be hit; tries to isolate you from your family and friends, then domestic violence is an element in your case.

- ❑ Make certain that every physical incident is documented by filing a police report. Obtain copies of all reports and make sure it is comprehensive and includes the follow-up Detective interview and comments. Make sure the report accurately states the details that you reported, if not, make sure the report is corrected until it completely and accurately describes the incident. If the incident resulted in a hospital visit, obtain a copy of the hospital report as well. Attending Physicians record in-detail statements from the patient and the physical demeanor of the patient. This hospital report will provide additional support and help substantiate the related police report. NEVER leave minor children with a perpetrator when going to the hospital after an altercation. This will likely have negative repercussions to your side of the case.

- ❑ Have all wounds and/or bruises photographed with a camera that records the date onto the photograph. Make sure family members or a close friend observes the wound and/or bruises to add credibility to your evidence.

The judicial system heavily scrutinizes violence in the home, especially if it occurs <u>in the presence of minor children.</u>

KEEP ALL ABOVE EVIDENCE IN A SAFE KEEPING PLACE OUTSIDE OF THE HOME.

Securing a Negotiation Style Attorney

It is strongly recommended that you and your spouse have separate legal representation. The dissolution of a marriage/family entity is a business transaction and should be treated as such. Your Attorney, Accountant and Therapist can advise you on your most favorable terms for a financial and custodial settlement.

- Prepare the following draft documents yourself if you wish to save funds on potential legal fees.

    - A one-page document itemizing the key elements of your case including key issues and concerns you have that need to be addressed

    - Prepare in advance all the questions you have regarding your case including the following key questions if applicable:

        If infidelity is an element in your case, ask the Attorney if it is relevant to the financial or child custody settlement to your case. If so, ask if they recommend the expense of a Private Investigator to produce an evidential report.

        If addiction or substance abuse is an element in your case, ask the Attorney if it is relevant to the financial or child custody settlement to your case. If so, do they recommend collecting evidence, what form of evidence do they recommend and who should collect the evidence (you or an investigator).

    Your draft proposed mediated contract including proposed financial settlement*and custodial parenting plan* if applicable. You can download very generic versions of these documents from your county government website that will require customizing to your case by your Attorney. Do not share these drafts with your spouse prior to a formal mediation, present these via your Attorney or in the mediation session in order to be the most productive in securing the terms that you would like.

*   *DO NOT USE YOUR HOME COMPUTER TO PREPARE OR STORE THESE DRAFTS. Store your drafted documents on a zip drive that you can provide to your Attorney to edit. This will save you substantial legal fees.*

- [ ] Select an Attorney *that someone you know recommends*. Gather your notebook, all compelling related evidence, and the above referenced drafted documents and take all to meet with several Attorneys for a complimentary consultation prior to securing an Attorney. *Seek referrals for Attorneys and only work with one who you know has been reasonable in their fee structure and productive for someone you know.* Hire the Attorney you feel understands your case the best and who is receptive to an immediate mediation. Ideally they should have experience in court (should your case require a hearing). They should be easy for you to communicate with. Flat fee firms will save you the most amount of money. Have the flat fees quoted in advance based on the various stages of representation outlined in the Average Timeline of Divorce Process in the beginning of this workbook. **Do not provide any financial information to an Attorney prior to getting fees quoted**. Document quoted fees in any contract you sign with your Attorney. Firmly insist on a mediation date to be set prior to the first conference date set with your Judge. This will minimize the risk of assets disappearing or a long drawn-out case that leaves you vulnerable to incurring unnecessary legal expenses and settling for far less than the law provides you are due.

At the beginning of your consultation, give your prepared case summary to the Attorney, ask them to read it before you start your discussion and sit silent while they do. This will help you make the most productive time of the consultation.

While interviewing your perspective Attorney, seek answers to the following key questions:

- [ ] Have you ever handled a case like mine with the listed specific variables on your one-page case summary?

- [ ] How do you usually communicate with your clients?

- [ ] Are you flat fee or billable hour billing based? What retainer fee do you require?

- [ ] Do you prefer to go to court or negotiate out of court?

- [ ] How many cases have you settled in the past 12 months, how many required a hearing or trial to be settled?

- [ ] What specific steps would you take in handling a case like mine?

- [ ] Can you provide me 2 to 3 names of former clients that I can speak with regarding your services?

Attorneys who settle most of their cases through trial will cost the most amount of money ($50,000+). A negotiation/mediation driven Attorney who avoids a trial should be able to settle your case for $10,000-$15,000.

Consideration of Mediation versus Litigation/Trial

Mediation is the most effective way to reach a settlement that meets the needs of all parties involved. Who best to make final decisions on your family but you and your spouse, taking your minor children into consideration? Why leave these important decisions to a Judge via a trial who already resents the fact that two married people can't be civilized enough to work out a reasonable arrangement? The Judicial System in Civil cases is designed to uphold the laws of the state in which you reside regarding the dissolution of the family entity. It is not designed to pass judgment or punish individuals on moral or ethical issues. It is important to address emotional issues in family counseling and not expect the judicial process to hold individuals accountable for their choice of behaviors that lead to the breakdown of the relationship. In many cases Litigator style Attorneys will feed off of the emotional aspects of your case, promising punishment and accountability simply to increase billable hours. Save family funds by eliminating the emotional aspect while in the legal arena. Trials are very costly and result in big paydays for Litigators, full days of depositions are required prior to the trials and a trial could take several days, costing your family many hours of unnecessary legal expenses that can range from an additional $5,000-$15,000+. If you have a lot of conflict in your marriage, a mediation where the parties are separated in different rooms can be very productive. Your Attorney can attend the mediation with you.

1 Week Prior to Your Attorney filing your case for divorce

- ❏ If possible without creating suspicion, start to update your Will, Power of Attorney, Living Will and all Beneficiaries of your personal Life Insurance policy and any financial assets based on how you want things to be handled once process is completed. Keep these updated documents in a safe place and give a complete set to a family member and to your Attorney.

- ❏ You must have all your preparation in this workbook completed before the suit is filed to maximize a swift and speedy process

- ❏ Once your finalized divorce documents are prepared by your Attorney/served to spouse:

  - ○ immediately secure any needed affidavits of all witnesses outside of family members (if relevant to your settlement)

  - ○ Have Attorney subpoena any banking or financial records you are missing. Financial institutions usually take 60-90 days to respond which can hold up your case and could cost you unnecessary legal fees, so it is important for you to gather all information that you possibly can yourself.

  - ○ Set a mediation date within 30-45 days. Once your case is filed, the court system requires 60 day status conferences with the Judge until you have reached a settlement. Every conference is very costly (Counsel usually bills 4-8 hours of time for each conference, which will cost your family $2400-$5000). It is in your family's best financial interest to invest these same funds in several productive mediations to settle your case as quickly as you can.

©2010 Transitions Resource | All rights reserved

How to Tell the Children

Denise Houston, Licensed Professional Counselor advises:

Parents should tell the children together if they can do so without volatility, blaming each other or defending themselves. A professional can coach parents and help them practice and prepare for this. Use statements such as:
"We will get along better if we live in separate houses"
"Parents do not divorce children, we are not divorcing you"
"We will both still love you and spend time with you"
"The divorce is not your fault"
"We will keep as many things the same as we possibly can (school, neighborhood, friends, etc.) "

Kathleen Shack, Marriage and Family Therapist adds:

Timing is important for children, tell them no more than 2 weeks before one of the parents moves out of the home. Also be prepared for questions, some popular questions include:
"Why did you stop loving Mommy/Daddy?" (disguised as "Will you stop loving me")
"Will you ever get back together?" (must be told very clearly that you will not be getting back together)
"Why did you break up our family?" (do not discuss the details with the kids, avoid assigning blame)
"Do I have to go to Mom's/Dad's?" (children need parenting time with both parents, work together to resolve)
"Am I getting a new Mom/Dad?" (no, parents are not replaceable)
"Where will I live?" (know the living arrangements prior to telling the kids, know the schedule)

❑ Place children into "family-in-transition" counseling immediately after suit is filed. This important step will help your children understand the changes in your family, give them a healthy perspective on the changes as well as an outlet to vent frustrations or concerns.

Safe Assumptions

If you discover through this process your spouse has secrets (hidden assets and/or money, infidelity, addictions) assume that your personal computer may have spy-ware installed tracking all of your computer activity. Individuals who keep secrets from their spouse go to unusual lengths to protect their secrets and can be highly suspicious or paranoid they may be discovered. Only correspond on your computer as if you know they are reading every correspondence. Do not do any divorce/separation/investigation research on your home computer. You can go to the local library to use on-line computers and read related self-help books.

Assume your spouse has keys to your car, access to all of your personal belongings, and may be reading all of your mail.

If you own a sophisticated smartphone software that may have been downloaded onto it allows others to hear your calls, see your text messages, emails, photographs and files and track your location, it can remotely be turned on so conversations around the phone can be heard. If you suspect your phone contains this software, purchase an inexpensive trac phone to conduct confidential conversations with your Attorney and others.

ONCE CASE IS SETTLED BE AWARE OF THE FOLLOWING:

Social Security Benefits:

If you were married 10 years or more, you and any minor children under the age of 18 may be eligible for Social Security benefits upon your ex-spouse retiring or becoming disabled prior to retiring. See resources for national Social Security office hotline number.

Minor Children as Beneficiaries:

Children under the legal age of 18 cannot legally manage any inheritance assets. Seek the counsel of an Attorney when updating your will as to how to set up a custodial account as beneficiary by creating a Trust. This will eliminate unnecessary Probate Court fees.

Change Beneficiaries:

Make sure to update beneficiaries and remove spouse on all IRA's, Banking accounts including Money Markets and Certificate of Deposits, 401ks and Life Insurance policies.

LIST OF DOCUMENTS TO GATHER– EXHIBIT A

(Place originals in safe keeping place, keep multiple copies at home/ friend/family)

- ☐ Your birth certificate
- ☐ Birth certificates of your children
- ☐ Your social security card
- ☐ Social security cards of your children
- ☐ Current copy of your and your spouse's social security benefit statement
- ☐ Your passport
- ☐ Passports for your children
- ☐ Marriage license
- ☐ Insurance policies (home/auto/life)
- ☐ Any legal separation documents (financial/custodial agreements)
- ☐ Police reports, photos of bruises/injuries if domestic violence related
- ☐ Hospital reports of above related incidents
- ☐ Medical reports/files, insurance claims if related to domestic violence
- ☐ Wills for You and your spouse, Power of Attorney, Living Will, Trust documents
- ☐ Credit card information/most recent credit report
- ☐ Loan/mortgage Information
- ☐ Bankruptcy discharge statement (if applicable)
- ☐ Complete copies of tax returns for the past 3 years (including all schedules)
- ☐ Titles of automobiles, boats
- ☐ Home deed or rental agreement
- ☐ Complete set of photographs of furniture and valuable collections, jewelry
- ☐ An extra set of keys to your automobile and home
- ☐ A current monthly pay stub from spouse's employment
- ☐ Comprehensive list of all known banking accounts, investment accounts and financial accounts, retirement accounts, IRA and work related savings/stock option plans (make sure list includes where account is held, account number and average value)
- ☐ A notebook compiling copies of all of these documents
    - Keep these in a safe place outside of the home.
    - Have a section with tables for each individual financial account and put accumulative copies of every monthly, quarterly or annual statement for the accounts in this notebook. A comprehensive history of these accounts is important.

FAMILY MONTHLY BUDGET WORKSHEET

	Jan	Feb	Mar	Apr	May	Jun	Jul	Aug	Sep	Oct	Nov	Dec
Home:												
Mortgage												
Prop tax												
Maintenance												
Insurance												
Electricity												
Gas												
Telephone												
Cell phone												
TV cable												
Water/sew												
Security Alarm												
Lawn care												
Waste												
Groceries												
Eating Out												
Entertain												
Med co-pay												
Eye care												
Medical Ins												
Clothes												
Vacations												
Pet Exp												
Auto:												
Insurance												
Prop tax												
Gas												
Children:												
Med Insurance												
Med co-pay												
Eye care												
Childcare												
Summer activ.												
Clothes												
School												
Extra curric.												

©2010 Transitions Resource | All rights reserved

FAMILY ASSET/NET WORTH WORKSHEET

Assets:			My Records		Spouse Provided	
Name of Bank						
Type	Acct #		date	$	date	$
Type	Acct #		date	$	date	$
Type	Acct #		date	$	date	$
Name of Bank						
Type	Acct #					
Type	Acct #		date	$	date	$
Type	Acct #		date	$	date	$
Investments:						
Name of Source:						
Type	Acct #		date	$	date	$
Type	Acct #		date	$	date	$
Retirement Savings:						
IRA	Acct #		date	$	date	$
401(k)	Acct #		date	$	date	$
Empl Savings	Acct #		date	$	date	$
Employee Stock Purchase:			date	$	date	$
Severance Offering			date	$		
Employee Pensions:						
Company			date	$	date	$
Company			date	$	date	$
Family Vehicle			date	$	date	$
Family Vehicle			date	$	date	$
Family Boat			date	$	date	$
Equity in Family Home			date	$	date	$
Totals:				$		$
Discrepancy						
Debt:						
Mortgage			date	$		
Credit Cards			date	$		
Home Equity Line of Credit			date	$		
Other loans/debts			date	$		
Family Net Worth:				$		

©2010 Transitions Resource | All rights reserved

Financial Considerations regarding Divorce Settlements:

Attorneys are licensed to advise and practice the laws in the state in which they reside and hold licensure in. **Attorneys are not licensed to give financial advice** *and can risk losing their legal license if they do so. Before one enters into financial negotiations or mediation for a financial divorce settlement it is wise to* **seek the advice of a licensed CPA and/or Tax Advisor** *regarding the particular details of their family situation and potential financial/tax implications of what they are considering for final settlement terms. Below are some points of discussion and consideration a CPA and/or Tax Advisor can assist with.*

Medical Insurance/Auto Insurance for minor children:
After securing quotes, discuss creative options for Medical Insurance/Auto Insurance coverage of minor children, which parent should carry minor children on their policy to minimize the expense to the new post-divorce family structure and how the expense should be structured proportionately based on parent income.

Division of Tax Deferred Retirement Accounts (401(k), Retirement Savings)
A majority of retirement accounts are pre-tax accounts. What this means is that any money you take out of the account will be subject to income tax. Therefore, the immediate cash values of these accounts are actually less than what the balance is. If you are younger than 59 ½, in most cases, an early distribution from a pre-tax retirement account will cost you a 10% penalty for an early withdraw in addition to income taxes. To transfer tax-deferred retirement account funds, a legal document called a Qualified Domestic Relations Order (QDRO) signed by your Judge is required authorizing the holding/manager of the funds to move the funds into separate accounts. The verbiage for this legal document must be supplied by the Corporation who is offering the retirement account and the preparation of these forms should be handled by an Attorney. Since there are legal expenses related to the preparation and filing of this document, the parties should address how this expense will be handled in their financial settlement agreement.

Transfer of Stock Holdings and potential tax liability if liquidated within 12 months of division of funds
If you acquire stock from your former spouse, you should understand the tax impact of cashing out the stocks. If you decide to sell the stock less than a year after you acquired it, the stock will be subject to income taxes (taxed at a maximum 35% rate through 2012). However, if the stock is held for a year or more, it will be taxed as a long term capital gain which has a much lower tax rate which is capped at 15% through 2012. Consider having names of both spouses added to the stock accounts prior to the division of the stocks if possible (during temporary settlement period).

Remember to consider the value of Retirement Pensions and Corporate Stock Options not yet exercised that accumulated during the marriage, these are considered marital assets.

Former Wills/ Trusts Documents/Marriage Licenses and Divorce Decrees
Post –Divorce it is important to retain **all originals** and **additional certified copies** of all of the above listed documents. Often, in order to obtain retirement benefits, Social Security benefits and Death benefits of an Ex-Spouse originals or certified copies of the above specified documents are required. If the partners were married for 10 years or more, Spouses are eligible for Ex-Spouse Social Security benefits beginning at age 60.

Below are some possible creative ways to distribute assets in a divorce that can be mutually beneficial to both parties. **Ensure you contact your CPA to confirm the tax benefits in your situation.** Also, confirm your Divorce Decree clearly outlines any implemented strategy.

1. legal fees (i.e., divorce attorney fees) are tax deductible against alimony received (have the legal fee bill itemize this) - have the one receiving the alimony pay the legal fees; share the resulting tax savings.

If you:
1. **Received alimony payments** (child support payments are not applicable to this deduction)
2. **Personally paid a Divorce Attorney**

there is a good probability you, or the person you know, is **due a tax refund/deduction** (if you/they have not already received one). If the deduction outlined below was missed, it may well be worth going back and re-filing a previous year tax return to capture the tax deduction.

As an example, your "work" income was $35,000/year and you received $24,000/year in alimony payments. The Divorce Attorney bill that <u>you</u> **(the alimony receiver)** paid was $22,000. Presume $1,000 of the $22,000 was to file the actual divorce papers and thus **$21,000 was paid by you to a Divorce Attorney to secure alimony.**

Here is a rough outline of your potential tax savings/refund (of course your actual numbers will be different):

Total income = $59,000 (i.e., $35,000 + $24,000 = $59,000)
Adjusted Gross Income (AGI) = $50,000 (presumes $9,000 in exemptions/deductions to get to AGI)
Schedule "A" standard deduction of 2% = $1,000 (i.e., 2% of $50,000 = $1,000)
Presume 25% Federal tax and 6% State tax

Your savings/refund = **($21,000 - $1,000)** X (25% + 6%) = **$6,200**

The following excerpts are taken from www.lawyers.com.
General Rules
The general rule is simple enough: You can deduct attorney's fees you pay for:
- Trying to produce or collect taxable income **(alimony is taxable income)**, or
- To help in determining, collecting or getting a refund of any tax
In simple terms, you can take a deduction if you need an attorney's help to make money **(alimony)** you have to pay taxes on

Is There a Deduction?
There are all kinds of situations that qualify for the tax deduction, such as fees you may pay for:
- **Tax advice** you may get during a divorce case, such as how you and your ex-spouse will take deductions for home mortgage interest or child care, or whether alimony is tax deductible by the payor spouse or taxable income to the recipient spouse
- **Trying to get your ex-spouse to pay past-due alimony**

What IRS Tax Form To Use
Generally, you deduct attorney's fees as an itemized miscellaneous deduction on Schedule A of your Form 1040 tax return. You may not be able to deduct all of your fees, though. Miscellaneous deductions are limited by the **two percent rule**: You can deduct only the amount of your miscellaneous deductions that's more than two percent of your **adjusted gross income** (AGI) - the amount you entered on line 38 of your 1040.

Check with Your Lawyer
If you're concerned about whether you'll be able to deduct attorney's fees, you can always ask your attorney - **before** she does any work for you - if any of the fees she'll charge are tax deductible.
Also, ask your attorney to prepare a billing a statement that shows clearly what part of her fees is deductible **(i.e., all the hours billable to secure alimony; which may be all of it except the filing fees)**. So, for example, if you're involved in a divorce, your lawyer's billing statement should show how much time she spent working on how the divorce will impact your taxes. It should be separate from the other nontax divorce issues, like the time spent drafting the divorce papers.

2. A direct distribution from an IRA or 401-K per the QDRO is not hit with the 10% IRS penalty.

©2010 Transitions Resource | All rights reserved

3. Have the higher income earner each year claim all the kids as dependents on his/her tax return each share - share the "net" tax savings equally via a check from the high income earner to the lower income earner.

As an example, presume the high income earner has a marginal Federal tax rate of 34% plus 6% State whereas the lower income earner has a Federal tax rate of 15% plus 6% State. Presume the standard child deduction is $3,700 (it changes most years) and there are 3 children.

- The higher income earner would save [(34% + 6%) X $3,700 X 3 = $4,440]
- The lower income earner would save [(15% + 6%) X $3,700 X 3 = $2,331]
- The annual tax savings differential in this case is $4,440 - $2,331 = $2,109
- The average between the two is $3,385.50
- The higher income earner would claim all 3 dependents and then write a check to the lower income earner for [($3,385.50 / 2) = $1,692.75]
- Over 2 years, instead of the high income earner getting a $4,440 tax savings year one and then $0 in year two (because the spouse claims the dependents) for a **total of $4,440**, the high income earner would get ($4,440 - $1,692.75) + ($4,440 - $1,692.75) = **$5,494.50**. Note this is an <u>extra tax savings of $1,054.50</u> compared to alternating claiming dependents.
- Over 2 years, instead of the low income earner getting a $0 tax savings year one (because the spouse claims the dependents) and then $2,331 in year two for a **total of $2,331**, the low income earner would get ($1,692.75) + ($1,692.75) = **$3,385.50**. Note this is an <u>extra tax savings of $1,054.50</u> compared to alternating claiming dependents.

To determine the exact tax savings differential each year, once each person's tax return is completed run a "dummy" version whereby the only adjustment to each person's tax return is eliminating the dependents, or adding the dependents, as the case may be. Then look at what the combined Federal plus State tax differential is for each of you. The higher income earner would then write a check for half of the net savings to the lower income earner.

4. If one of the parties will have a higher income tax bracket than the other after the divorce, consider settling non-qualified accounts, home equity, and other non-qualified asset splits as "enhanced" alimony payments (from the high income earner to the low income earner) versus a lump sum settlement. Increase/enhance the "alimony" amount to cover the alimony receiver's tax burden and share equally in the "net" tax deduction savings of the higher income earner.

As an example, presume a couple had $200,000 in equity in a home to be shared equally (change the amount to fit your scenario). Instead of each party taking $100,000 (with no tax implications) consider:

- the high income earner keeps his/her $100,000 with no adjustment.
- the high income earner pays the low income earner more than $100,000 (as outlined below) in alimony over 3 years (or whatever duration you mutually choose). Be cognizant that this extra income does not push the low income earner into a higher tax bracket or lower the higher income earner into a lower tax bracket; if it does, adjust accordingly.
- Presume the higher income earner is in the (34% + 6%) = 40% Federal plus State tax bracket. Change the numbers to fit your scenario.
- Presume the lower income earner is in the (15% + 6%) 21% Federal plus State tax bracket. Change the numbers to fit your scenario.
- Note: the greater the difference between the 2 tax brackets, the greater the benefit of this strategy
- To calculate the fair payment amount to each, net of taxes, here is the formula whereby
  - A = the amount of the lower income earner's share to be "converted" to alimony
  - H = the higher income earners Federal plus State tax bracket
  - L = the lower income earners Federal plus State tax bracket
  - (A X 2) / [(1 – H) + (1 – L)]
  - So in this example:
  - ($100,000 X 2) / [(1 - 0.4) + (1 - 0.21)] = $200,000 / (0.6 + 0.79) = $143,885
- The higher income earner would thus pay the lower income earner $143,885 / 3 = $47,962/year for 3 years. This payment should be made in lump sum the first week of January each year.
- The higher income earner gets a cumulative tax break of ($143,885 X 40%) = $57,554
  - Thus, net of taxes, the high income earner pays
  - $143,885 - $57,554 = $86,331
  - compared to paying $100,000 with no tax savings; for a net savings of $13,669
- The lower income earner incurs a cumulative increased tax of ($143,885 X 21%) = $30,216
  - Thus, net of taxes, the low income earner receives
  - $143,885 - $30,216 = $113,669
  - compared to receiving $100,000 with no taxes; for a net increase of $13,669
- As result of this strategy, in this example, **each** party has an **extra $13,669**.

SAMPLE PARENTING PLAN- Exhibit B

This document is not to be construed as legal advice. Seek a Licensed Attorney in your state to provide an appropriate document for your case. This is only a general example of what a parenting plan would include.

Petitioner: _____

Respondent: _____

Civil Action # _____

PARENTING PLAN

☐ The parties have agreed to the terms of this plan and this information has been furnished by both parties to meet the requirements of OCGA §19-9-1. The parties agree on the terms of the plan and affirm the accuracy of the information provided, as shown by their signatures at the end of this Order.

☐ This plan has been prepared by the Judge.
This plan
☐ is a new plan
☐ modifies an existing Parenting Plan dated _____.
☐ modifies an existing Order dated _____.

CHILD'S NAME   BIRTHDATE
_____   _____
_____   _____

I. CUSTODY AND DECISION MAKING

A. LEGAL CUSTODY (choose one):

☐ with the mother
☐ with the father
☐ joint custody

B. PRIMARY PHYSICAL CUSTODY

NAME	BIRTHDATE	MOTHER	FATHER	JOINT
_____	_____	☐	☐	☐
_____	_____	☐	☐	☐

WHERE JOINT PHYSICAL CUSTODY IS CHOSEN BY THE PARENTS OR ORDERED BY THE COURT, A DETAILED PLAN OF THE LIVING ARRANGEMENTS OF THE CHILD(REN) SHALL BE ATTACHED AND MADE A PART OF THIS PARENTING PLAN.

C. DAY TO DAY DECISIONS

Each parent shall make decisions regarding day to day care of a child while the child is residing with the parent, including any emergency decisions affecting the   health or safety of a child.

D. MAJOR DECISIONS

Major decisions regarding each child shall be made as follows:

Education   ☐ mother ☐ father ☐ joint
Non-emergency health care   ☐ mother ☐ father ☐ joint
Religious upbringing   ☐ mother ☐ father ☐ joint
Extracurricular activities   ☐ mother ☐ father ☐ joint
Psychological decisions   ☐ mother ☐ father ☐ joint
_____   ☐ mother ☐ father ☐ joint

©2010 Transitions Resource | All rights reserved

E. DISAGREEMENTS

Where parents have elected joint decision making in Section I. D. above, please explain how any disagreements in decision making will be resolved, i.e., explain the process parents will use when a tie breaker is needed.

_____
_____

II. PARENTING TIME/VISITATION SCHEDULES

A. Parenting Time/Visitation

During the term of this Parenting Plan the non-custodial parent shall have at a minimum the following rights of parenting time/visitation (choose an item):

☐ The weekend of the first and third Friday of each month
☐ The weekend of the first, third, and fifth Friday of each month
☐ The weekend of the second and fourth Friday of each month.
☐ Every other weekend starting on _____.
☐ Each _____ starting at _____am/pm and ending at _____ am/pm
☐ Other: _____ ☐ and weekday parenting time/ visitation on (choose an item):
　　☐ none
　　☐ every Wednesday evening.
　　☐ every other Wednesday evening during the week prior to a non-　visitation weekend
　　☐ every _____ and _____ evening.
　　☐ other: _____
_____

For purposes of this Parenting Plan, a weekend will start at _____am/pm on (circle one) Thursday/Friday/Saturday/Other: _____ and end at _____am/pm on (circle one) Sunday/Monday/Other:_____.

Weekday visitation will begin at _____am/pm and will end at (circle one) _____am/pm/ when the child(ren) return(s) to school or day care the next morning/Other:_____
_____
_____.

This parenting schedule begins (check one):
☐ _____ OR ☐ on the date of the Court's Order.
　　(date and time)

B. MAJOR HOLIDAYS AND VACATION PERIODS

THANKSGIVING

The day to day schedule shall apply unless other arrangements are set forth: _____
beginning _____.

WINTER VACATION

The (choose one) ☐ mother ☐ father shall have the child(ren) for the first period from the day and time school is dismissed until December _____ at _____am/pm in (choose one) ☐ odd numbered years ☐ even numbered years ☐ every year. The other parent will have the child(ren) for the second period from the day and time indicated above until 6:00 pm on the evening before school resumes. Unless otherwise indicated, the parties shall alternate the first and seconds periods each year.

Other agreement of the parents: _____
_____

SUMMER VACATION:

Define summer vacation period. Include an explanation of the way that summer camp will be addressed, if applicable. For example, will visitation take priority over camp? If visitation is one week on and one week off, will camp be one week on and one week off?
_____
_____

The day to day schedule shall apply unless other arrangements are set forth:
_____beginning
_____

SPRING VACATION (if applicable):

Define: _____
_____

The day to day schedule shall apply unless other arrangements are set forth:
_____
_____beginning
_____.

FALL VACATION (if applicable):

Define: _____
_____

The day to day schedule shall apply unless other arrangements are set forth:
_____
_____

beginning _____.

C. OTHER HOLIDAY SCHEDULE (if applicable):

Indicate if the child(ren) will be with the parent in ODD or EVEN numbered years or EVERY year:

	MOTHER	FATHER	
Martin Luther King Day			
President's Day			
Mother's Day			
Memorial Day			
Father's Day			
July Fourth			
Labor Day			
Halloween			
Child(ren)'s Birthday			
Mother's Birthday			
Father's Birthday			
Religious Holiday:			
Religious Holiday:			
Religious Holiday:			
Religious Holiday:			
Other:			
Other:			
Other:			

D. OTHER EXTENDED PERIODS OF TIME DURING SCHOOL, ETC. (REFER TO THE SCHOOL SCHEDULE)

_____

E. START AND END DATES FOR HOLIDAY VISITATION:

For the purposes of this Parenting Plan, the holiday will start and end as follows (choose one):
☐ Holidays that fall on Friday will include the following Saturday and Sunday
☐ Holidays that fall on Monday will include the preceding Saturday and Sunday
☐ Other: _____
_____

F. COORDINATION OF PARENTING SCHEDULES

Check if applicable:
☐ The holiday parenting time/visitation schedule takes precedence over the regular parenting time/visitation schedule.

☐ When the child(ren) is/are with a parent for an extended parenting time/visitation period (such as summer), the other parent shall be entitled to visit with the child(ren) during the extended period, as follows:
_____
_____

G. TRANSPORTATION ARRANGEMENTS

For visitation, the place of the meeting for the exchange of the child(ren) shall be:
_____
_____

The _____ will be responsible for transportation of the child at the beginning of the visitation.

The _____ will be responsible for transportation of the child at the conclusion of the visitation.

Transportation costs, if any, will be allocated as follows:
_____
_____

Other provisions:_____
_____

H. CONTACTING THE CHILD

When the child(ren) is/are in the physical custody of one parent, the other parent will have the right to contact the child(ren) as follows:
☐ Telephone
☐ Other: _____
_____
☐ Limitations on contact: _____
_____

I. SUPERVISION OF PARENTING TIME (if applicable):

☐ Check here if applicable
Supervised parenting time shall apply during the day to day schedule as follows:

Place: _____
Person/Organization supervising: _____
Responsibility for cost (check one)   ☐ mother   ☐ father   ☐ both equally

J. COMMUNICATION PROVISIONS

Please check the applicable provision:

☐ Each parent shall promptly notify the other parent of a change in address, phone number or cell phone number. A parent changing residence must give at least 30 days notice of the change and provide the full address of the new residence.

©2010 Transitions Resource | All rights reserved

☐ Due to prior acts of family violence, the address of the child(ren) and victim of family violence shall be kept confidential. The protected parent shall promptly notify the other parent, through a third party, of any change in contact information necessary to conduct visitation.

III. ACCESS TO RECORDS AND INFORMATION

RIGHTS OF THE PARENTS

Absent agreement to limitations of court ordered limitations, pursuant to OCGA § 19-9-1(b)(1)(D), both parents are entitled to access to all of the child(ren)s records and information, including, but not limited to, education, health, extracurricular activities, and religious communications. Designation as a non- custodial parent does not affect a parent's right to equal access to these records.

Limitation on access rights: _____
_____
Other information sharing provisions: _____
_____

IV. MODIFICATION OF PLAN OR DISAGREEMENTS

Parties may, by mutual agreement, vary the parenting time/visitation; however, such agreement shall not be a binding Court Order. Custody shall only be modified by Court Order.

Should the parents disagree about this Parenting Plan or wish to modify it, they must make a good faith effort to resolve the issue between themselves.

V. SPECIAL CONSIDERATIONS

Please attach an addendum detailing any special circumstances of which the Court should be aware (e.g., health issues, educational issues, etc.)
_____
_____

VI. PARENT'S CONSENT

Please review the following and initial:

    1. We recognize that a close and continuing parent-child relationship and continuity in the child(ren)'s life is in the child(ren)'s best interest.

    Mother's Initial's_____   Father's Initial's _____

    2. We recognize that our child(ren)'s needs will change and grow as the child(ren) mature(s); we have made a good faith effort to take these changing needs into account so that the need for future modifications to the Parenting Plan is minimized.

    Mother's Initial's_____   Father's Initial's _____

    3. We recognize that the parent with physical custody will make the day to day decisions and emergency decisions while the child is residing with such parent.

    Mother's Initial's_____   Father's Initial's _____

☐ We knowingly and voluntarily agree on the terms of this Parenting Plan. Each of us affirms that the information we have provided in this Plan in true and correct.

_____   _____
Father's Signature   Mother's Signature

ORDER

The Court has reviewed the foregoing Parenting Plan, and it is hereby made the Order of the Court. This Order entered on _____, _____   _____
                                                   JUDGE

RESOURCES

Helpful Books and Articles

What do Divorce Lawyers do In their Own Divorces-Huffpost 2/9/2012- Kulerski & Cornelison
The High Road Has Less Traffic-Monique A. Honaman
Verbal Abuse Survivors Speak Out – Patricia Evans
Hanging on by My Fingernails, *How a Scratch Can Land You in Jail* – Janie McQueen
When Dad Hurts Mom – Lundy Bancroft
Splitting – Protecting Yourself While Divorcing a Narcissist – Bill Eddy
The Betrayal Bond, Breaking Free of Exploitive Relationships – Carnes
Deceived, Facing Sexual Betrayal, Lies and Secrets – Claudia Black
Mending a Shattered Heart – Carnes

Spiritual Based Books

God Calling – A.J. Russell
Why? – Anne Graham Lotz
Fool-Proofing Your Life – Jan Silvious

Support Groups and Organizations

AL-ANON – www.ola-is.org
Smartrecovery.org
CODA – Codependents Anonymous, www.codependents.org
GCADV- Coalition Against Domestic Violence, www.GCADV.org
COSA- Codependents of Individuals with Compulsive Sexual Behavior, www.cosa-recovery.org
S-ANON – Codependents of Sexaholics, www.sanon.org
SRA – Sexual Recovery Anonymous, www.sexualrecovery.org
RCA – Recovering Couples Anonymous, www.recovery-couples.org
L.I.F.E. – Christian-based "sexual addiction recovery community"

Background Checks Online

www.ussearch.com

Credit Report Online:

www.Equifax.com – 2 per year for free

Social Security Office

1-800-772-1213

Made in the USA
Lexington, KY
30 June 2016